GW01045096

from confetti.co.uk
don't get married without us...

First published in 2003 by Octopus Publishing Group,
2–4 Heron Quays, London E14 4JP
www.conran-octopus.co.uk

A catalogue record for this book is available
from the British Library.

ISBN 184091 307 X

Publishing Director Lorraine Dickey
Senior Editor Katey Day
Assistant Editor Sybella Marlow
Creative Director Leslie Harrington
Designer Jeremy Tilston
Senior Production Controller Manjit Sihra

Contents

In the weird and wonderful world of weddings, there are countless traditions from across centuries and continents. What is not done in one part of the world is essential in another, what was frowned on in one year was praised in another. Each week Aunt Betti, Confetti's agony aunt, receives many emails requesting clarification of the myriad wedding traditions.

How to use this book

With a group of friends – pass the book around the group. Each person dips in and reads out a question. See who scores the highest!

On your own – covering the answers (on the bottom of the pages) with your thumbs, go through the questions in order. When you reach the end, check how many you got right. Turn to the scoring guide on page 126 to see how well you did!

How to use this book

On a hen night – test the bride's wedding knowledge. Turn it into a game by making her do a forfeit or dare for every answer she gets wrong!

On a hen night – split into teams and see which team scores the highest.

Have a bit of a laugh – some of the traditions are very odd indeed!

How not to use this book

Don't use this book to scare yourself into thinking that you are doing something that isn't traditional, or might be bad luck.

Don't use this book to scare yourself into thinking that you are not doing enough traditional things that will bring you good luck!

Just enjoy!

WEDDING TRIVIA

1. Which of Henry VIII's wives outlived him?

A: Katherine Parr
B: Catherine Howard
C: Anne of Cleves

Q: 1 = A

2. In the traditional saying 'something old, something new, something borrowed, something blue', what does something old represent?

A: the age of the groom
B: a link with the bride's old life
C: the age of the vicar

Q:2=B

WEDDING TRIVIA

3. To whom did Simone de Beauvoir
write her famous love letters?

A: Jean-Paul Sartre
B: Jean Paul Gaultier
C: Jean Paul II

THE QUIZ

4. In the context of a wedding, what is a favour?

A: a gift given to guests as a keepsake of the wedding

B: something the bride promises the groom on the wedding night

C: something given to the chief bridesmaid by the best man

Q:4=A

WEDDING TRIVIA

5. Where might you be married by Elvis?

A: Las Vegas
B: Los Angeles
C: Disney World

THE QUIZ

6. What's the difference between a bridesmaid and a matron of honour?

A: a matron of honour is always taller than the bridesmaids

B: matron of honour is the title given to a married chief bridesmaid

C: the matron of honour is the bride's best friend while bridesmaids should always be related to the bride

Q:6=B

7. Who should be first on the dance floor?

A: all the children, who should
be worn out early and then sent to bed
B: the groom's parents
C: the bride and groom

8. Who wrote 'The Marriage of Figaro'?

    A: Mozart
    B: Figaro
    C: Burt Bacharach

Q:8=A

9. Which document is it possible to
have amended to your married name
before the wedding?

A: the marriage certificate
B: your passport
C: your birth certificate

Q:9=B

THE QUIZ

10. In Greece, on which day do weddings almost always take place?

A: Sundays
B: bank holidays
C: rainy days

Q:10=A

11. What is the traditional gift for a first
wedding anniversary?

    A: scissors

    B: paper

    C: crayons

Q:11=B

12. Diamonds are graded using the four Cs.
What are they?

A: chicken, carrot, curry, chilli
B: cheap, cheerful, crazy, colourful
C: cut, clarity, colour, carat

Q:12=C

13. Why do guests traditionally tie shoes to the back of the newly weds' car?

A: as a symbol of fertility

B: in case they break down and have to continue on foot

C: to remind them where the boot is

14. Which colour is considered lucky in
association with a wedding?

    A: pink
    B: white
    C: blue

Q:14=C

15. Who traditionally sits either side of the
bride at the top table?

A: the mother and father of the bride
B: the best man and chief bridesmaid
C: the groom and father of the bride

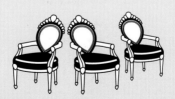

Q:15=C

16. What do the five sugar-coated almonds, traditionally given at weddings, symbolize?

A: Scary, Sporty, Posh, Baby and Ginger

B: health, wealth, fertility, happiness and long life

C: Monday, Tuesday, Wednesday, Thursday and Friday

Q:16=B

17. Why do Jewish couples stamp on a champagne glass during the ceremony?

A: because there are too many
B: to save on the washing up
C: for good luck

Q:17=C

THE QUIZ

18. Who said 'Men marry because they are tired; women because they are curious. Both are disappointed'?

A: Oscar Wilde
B: Kim Wilde
C: Ozzie Osbourne

Q:18=A

19. What is an ascot?

A: a type of cravat
B: a buttonhole
C: a hat

THE QUIZ

20. Church bells are rung at the end of a wedding ceremony to...

A: let all the townspeople know

B: wake those guests who have fallen asleep

C: drive away evil spirits

Q:20=C

WEDDING TRIVIA

21. What is the traditional gift for a
second wedding anniversary?

    A: cotton
    B: denim
    C: PVC

Q:21=A

22. Which bride firmly established white as the traditional colour for wedding dresses?

A: Queen Elizabeth II
B: Queen Victoria
C: Victoria Beckham

Q:22=B

23. What does 'morning dress' indicate?

A: wedding guests should turn up in their pyjamas

B: wedding guests should wear black

C: male guests should wear top hat and tails

24. During the marriage ceremony,
why does the bride traditionally
stand on the groom's left?

A: to leave his right hand free to
grab his sword
B: to leave his right hand free to
hold up the best man
C: so that he's nearest the exit

Q:24=A

25. In the traditional saying 'something old, something new, something borrowed, something blue', what does something borrowed represent?

A: an inability to balance the wedding budget

B: a sign that the bride's neighbours should lock up their lawnmower

C: good luck

26. Which language does the
word confetti come from?

    A: Dutch
    B: Welsh
    C: Italian

Q:26=C

27. In which country would the bride
traditionally wear red and gold?

> **A:** China
> **B:** USA
> **C:** Belgium

Q:27=A

28. What do Moroccan women bathe in
before the wedding ceremony?

> **A:** milk
> **B:** honey
> **C:** lemon juice

Q:28=A

29. What are banns?

A: the public declaration of an intended marriage

B: the entertainment for the reception

C: the traditional name for the rings exchanged during the ceremony

Q:29=A

30. Henry VIII changed the law to make it legal for which related persons to marry?

A: mother and son
B: brother and sister
C: cousins

Q:30=C

31. What is the top tier of the wedding cake traditionally saved for?

A: to throw at the bride and groom for luck

B: to be buried in the garden, then dug up and eaten on the first wedding anniversary

C: to be used as a christening cake for the couple's first child

Q:31=C

32. At a Scottish Penny wedding, what is it traditional to do to the bride on the eve of her marriage?

> **A:** tuck her into bed
> **B:** wash her feet
> **C:** give her a kiss

Q:32=B

33. What does the wedding cake symbolize?

    A: a bountiful kitchen

      B: fertility

    C: sexual appetite

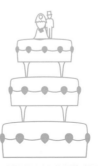

Q:33=B

34. What is traditionally thrown as the
bride and groom leave the church?

A: leaves

B: streamers

C: confetti

Q:34=C

35. What is the traditional gift on a third wedding anniversary?

    A: leather
    B: tin
    C: silk

36. What does a professional toastmaster do?

A: makes the toast for the wedding breakfast

B: organizes the toasters that have been given as wedding presents

C: acts as master of ceremonies to ensure the reception runs smoothly

WEDDING TRIVIA

37. Traditionally, why does the bride carry
a bouquet of flowers?

A: in ancient times the fragrance was
supposed to ward off evil spirits
B: to hide her stomach
C: to hit the groom with if he stumbled
over his vows

Q:37=A

38. What would the groom carry in his pocket at a traditional Italian wedding?

    A: a rabbit's foot
    B: a silver sixpence
    C: a piece of iron

Q:38=C

39. What is a bonbonniere?

A: an Italian wedding favour
B: a circular bouquet for a bridesmaid
C: a bustle attached to the back of a
wedding dress

40. Who wrote the words
'Love feels no burden...'?

A: Thomas à Kempis
B: Thomas Aquinas
C: Thomas à Becket

Q:40=A

WEDDING TRIVIA

41. According to the legend, with whom was Robin Hood in love?

A: Maid Marian
B: Mistress Melinda
C: Matronly Margaret

Q:41 =A

THE QUIZ

42. What is the supposed fate of the woman who catches the bride's bouquet?

A: her hay fever will be cured
B: she'll become pregnant
C: she'll be the next to marry

Q:42=C

43. In which country do people pinch the
bride for good luck?

A: Ireland
B: Egypt
C: Indonesia

Q:43=B

44. Shakespeare wrote 'Love looks not with the eyes, but with the...'

> **A:** heart
> **B:** mind
> **C:** binoculars

Q:44=B

45. In traditional Jewish weddings couples get married beneath a...?

A: Hanukkah
B: chuppah
C: mazeltov

46. Which one of these people does not traditionally sit at the top table?

A: groom
B: photographer
C: best man

Q:46=B

47. What do the following have in common:
dove, frog, goat, lizard and lamb?

A: they all make great main course
dishes for the wedding reception

B: they're all good omens if seen on
the way to the ceremony

C: they're all tied to the back of the
newly weds' car for luck

Q:47=B

48. What is the traditional gift for a
tenth wedding anniversary?

>   **A:** straw
>   **B:** fur
>   **C:** tin

Q:48=C

49. During the speeches, who traditionally thanks and toasts the bridesmaids?

A: the bridesmaids' parents

B: the groom

C: the toastmaster

Q:49=B

50. In Sweden, a bride puts a gold coin from her father in one shoe. What does her mother give her to put in the other?

A: a piece of bark

B: a pickled herring

C: a silver coin

Q:50=C

51. What is the wedding breakfast?

A: the last meal eaten by the bride
as a single woman, on the morning
of her wedding

B: the first meal eaten by the newly weds
on the morning after their wedding

C: the meal served at the reception
following the ceremony

Q:51=C

52. The Romans believed a kiss following
the marital vows...

A: would ensure lots of healthy children
B: was foreplay for later on
C: bound the couple's souls together

Q:52=C

WEDDING TRIVIA

53. Why does the bride traditionally
wear white?

A: as a symbol of prosperity
B: as a symbol of purity
C: as a symbol of poverty

Q:53=B

54. Which popular wedding flower means
'happiness in marriage'?

> **A:** red rose
> **B:** stephanotis
> **C:** pink lily

Q:54=B

55. Finish the next line: 'If thou must love me, then let it be for naught...'

A: Except for love's sake only
B: Unless we get a pony
C: I'm on to you – you phoney!

56. In which country might you attend a bridal shower?

A: USA
B: England
C: India

Q:56=A

57. Why does the groom carry his bride
over the threshold?

A: to protect her from evil spirits
B: because she's bound to get drunk
at the reception
C: to prove that he isn't as drunk as
she thinks he is

Q:57=A

58. Which British royal renounced the
throne to marry a divorcee?

A: Edward VIII
B: Edward the Confessor
C: Edward Earl of Wessex

Q:58=A

59. What is thrown at Czech newly weds instead of rice?

> **A:** peas
> **B:** peanuts
> **C:** seeds

60. What is the traditional gift for a fifteenth wedding anniversary?

A: linen
B: crystal
C: ink

Q:60=B

61. According to folklore, which month is said to be the unluckiest for weddings?

A: May

B: January

C: November

62. Which one of the following is not
a wedding tradition?

A: feeding the cat out of an old shoe
on the wedding day
B: preventing the bride and groom
from seeing each other on the morning
of the wedding
C: sipping milk fresh from the cow on
the morning of the wedding

Q:62=C

63. Why do Greek brides tuck a sugar cube into their glove?

A: because they're not sweet enough

B: they can eat it later when their energy is low

C: to sweeten the union in marriage

Q:63=C

THE QUIZ

64. What is behind the tradition of the
bride wearing something blue?

A: it represents the sadness she
feels on her wedding day
B: it shows total support for Everton
over Liverpool FC
C: it's a symbol of purity and fidelity

Q:64=C

65. Why does the bride wear a veil?

A: to prevent the congregation seeing
her crying

B: to stop the groom changing his mind

C: to protect her from evil spirits

Q:65=C

Over 60

May we offer you a hand in marriage? You've got the basics down, but now it's time to take it to the next level (without turning into a bridezilla, of course). Q. What's a Bridezilla? A. A control freak bride!

Under 60

Don't be misled by the word 'trivia' – some of this stuff's pretty useful to know! You don't want to find yourself setting off for the ceremony and realizing you don't know if the bridesmaids go in before or after the bride, or standing up at the reception not knowing what to say in your speech.

Fortunately www.confetti.co.uk is open 24 hours a day with all the answers you need.

ABOUT CONFETTI.CO.UK

Confetti.co.uk is the UK's leading weddings and special occasion website, helping more than 300,000 brides, grooms and guests every month.

To find out more or to order your confetti gift book, party brochure or wedding stationery brochure, visit www.confetti.co.uk email info@confetti.co.uk

visit Confetti, 80 Tottenham Court Road, London W1 or call 0870 840 6060

Some of the other books in this comprehensive series: *Compatibility, The Wedding Book of Calm, Confettiquette* and *Wedding Planner*

66. What is the origin of the receiving line?

A: it's based on American
line-dancing techniques

B: it allows the bride's father to
count up how much the reception
is likely to cost him

C: the belief that it's lucky for the guests
to touch the bridal party

Q:66=C

67. Who usually travels in the car with
the bridesmaids?

A: the bride
B: the groom
C: the mother of the bride

Q:67=C

THE QUIZ

68. What is reportage?

A: a traditional French wedding cake
B: a style of photography popular
at weddings
C: the traditional name for the bride's
going away outfit

Q:68=B

69. What is the traditional gift for a twentieth wedding anniversary?

A: plastic

B: china

C: paper

Q:69=B

70. What is meant by the term
'bottom drawer'?

A: a collection of items such as linen, for
the bride to start off married life

B: an assortment of underwear pinned
to the bride on her hen night

C: a collection of magazines, which the
groom must dispose of after the wedding

Q:70=A

71. Whose job is it to arrange
the stag night?

A: the bride's
B: the best man's
C: the vicar's

72. Who traditionally pays for the
wedding reception?

A: the bride's father
B: the groom's father
C: the vicar

Q:72=A

73. Which of the following would not be
allowed at a civil wedding ceremony?

A: hymns
B: readings
C: vows

THE QUIZ

74. In the traditional saying 'something old, something new, something borrowed, something blue', what does something new represent?

A: good fortune and success in the bride's new life

B: the size of the groom's bank account

C: the size of the bride's overdraft

Q:74=A

75. The original reason to have a
best man was…

A: to ask for the bride's hand on behalf
of the groom
B: to defend the groom against anyone
who might try to steal his bride
C: to marry the bride at the last
minute if anything happened to
the groom on the way to
the ceremony

Q:75=B

76. Why do people throw rice or
confetti at weddings?

A: to make the photographs
more colourful
B: to symbolize fertility
C: to annoy the vicar

Q:76=B

77. What would the bride do with a
silver sixpence?

A: use it as a deposit for her dress
B: wear it in her shoe for luck
C: give it to the groom as a
wedding present

78. During the speeches, whose role is it to thank the parents?

    A: the chief bridesmaid's
      B: the caterer's
      C: the groom's

Q:78=C

79. Who usually travels in the car
with the bride?

A: the vicar
B: the bride's father
C: the bridesmaids

Q:79=B

80. What is a dowry?

A: the money or property the bride
brings to the marriage
B: an open-top vintage car
C: a blessing of the marriage conducted
at Roman Catholic weddings

Q:80=A

81. What is a pre-nuptial agreement?

A: a contract between the bride and groom that outlines how their assets are distributed

B: a contract between the bride and her parents that lists which items she can take with her to the marital home

C: a contract that shows how many bottles of wine will be set out per table at the reception

82. What is the traditional gift for a
thirtieth wedding anniversary?

A: pearls
B: oysters
C: shells

Q:82=A

WEDDING TRIVIA

83. Complete the saying 'Three times a bridesmaid…'

A: always a bridesmaid

B: four times a wife

C: never a bride

Q:83=C

84. How would the bride traditionally
wear her rings?

A: the engagement ring goes on first
with the wedding ring on top
B: the wedding ring goes on first with
engagement ring on top
C: the wedding ring is worn on the left
hand, the engagement ring on the right

Q:84=A

85. What is a corsage?

A: a type of bridal headdress

B: a cravat worn by the groom

C: a small bunch of flowers worn
     pinned to the bodice

Q:85=C

86. A bride's bouquet traditionally includes which aromatic flower as a symbol of chastity?

A: orange blossom
B: banana blossom
C: orange squash

Q:86=A

87. Wedding cake has its origins in the ritual of breaking bread over a bride's head, a tradition that began in...

A: Egypt
B: Italy
C: Mexico

Q:87=B

88. What is significant about 29th February?

    A: it's a bank holiday

    B: it's pay day

    C: a woman can propose

    to a man on this day

Q:88=C

WEDDING TRIVIA

89. *The Wedding March* from Wagner's opera *Lohengrin* is better known as..?

A: Here Comes the Bride
B: There Goes the Groom
C: Where's the Vicar?

Q:89=A

90. What is the traditional gift for a fortieth wedding anniversary?

A: rubber
B: ruby
C: ribbon

Q:90=B

91. In the 17th century, an unmarried woman would place her piece of wedding cake under her pillow to...

A: save for a midnight feast
B: tempt an unsuspecting bachelor
C: improve her chances of finding a husband

Q:91=C

THE QUIZ

92. In the United Kingdom, what is the legal age for marriage?

A: 16, with parental consent
B: 18, with parental consent
C: 21

Q:92=A

93. Who wrote 'If music be the food of love, play on'?

A: William Shakespeare
B: William Shatner
C: Kenneth Williams

THE QUIZ

94. Who traditionally pays for
the honeymoon?

A: the best man
B: the groom
C: the travel agent

Q:94=B

95. With whom does the best man
traditionally dance?

A: the bride's mother
B: the groom's mother
C: the chief bridesmaid

Q:95=C

96. What is the bride's equivalent
of a stag party?

A: a stagette party
B: a hen party
C: a bridal party

Q:96=B

97. What does RSVP mean?

A: Return straight to vicar please
B: Répondez s'il vous plaît
C: Reception seating for vegetarian people

THE QUIZ

98. Which of these is part of a Chinese wedding celebration?

A: the noodle dance
B: the chopstick duel
C: the tea ceremony

Q:98=C

99. What are showers, teardrops and posies?

A: types of veil
B: good luck charms
C: styles of bouquet

Q:99=C

100. How much did Queen Victoria's wedding cake weigh?

> **A:** 100 lb
> **B:** 200 lb
> **C:** 300 lb

Q:100=C

101. What is the traditional gift for a forty-fifth wedding anniversary?

> **A:** emerald
> **B:** pearl
> **C:** sapphire

THE QUIZ

102. In Holland, a pine tree planted outside the newly weds' home is a symbol of...

A: fertility
B: nature
C: future firewood

Q:102=A

103. At a civil wedding, who makes the final decision on the ceremony content?

A: a detective superintendent
B: a registered superintendent
C: a superintendent registrar

Q:103=C

104. What is a croquembouche?

A: a type of cravat traditionally worn
by the groom
B: a headdress made of fresh flowers and
worn by the youngest bridesmaid
C: a traditional French wedding cake

Q:104=C

105. What is the traditional gift for a fiftieth wedding anniversary?

A: gold
B: silver
C: bronze

Q:105=A

106. A woman may not marry her...

A: brother's best friend
B: uncle
C: cousin

Q:106=B

107. How many of Henry VIII's wives
escaped being beheaded?

A: four
B: three
C: two

THE QUIZ

108. On which finger is the wedding ring worn?

A: the third finger of the left hand
B: the index finger of the right hand
C: the thumb on either hand

Q:108=A

109. Complete this line from a well-known sonnet 'Shall I compare thee to a summer's…'

A: night
B: afternoon
C: day

THE QUIZ

110. What did Roman brides carry instead of flowers?

> **A:** money
> **B:** herbs
> **C:** cloth

Q:110=B

111. During the speeches, whose role is it to talk about the groom?

A: the mother of the bride
B: the DJ
C: the best man

Q:111=C

112. What is the traditional gift for a
sixtieth wedding anniversary?

A: cubic zirconia
B: rhinestone
C: diamond

Q:112=C

WEDDING TRIVIA

113. What is the term used for the ritual
of raising a glass in honour of
the bride and groom?

> **A:** the roast
> **B:** the fry
> **C:** the toast

Q:113=C

114. Which of these may be worn
by the groom?

    A: an ascot
    B: a cassock
    C: a Cossack

        Q:114=A

115. Which sonnet begins
'Let me not to the marriage of true minds
Admit impediments; love is not love
Which alters when it alteration finds'?

A: Shakespeare's sonnet 116
B: Shakespeare's sonnet 18
C: Shakespeare's sonnet 127

116. Who should the groom ask for the bride's hand in marriage?

A: the bride's father
B: the bride's boss
C: the bride's best friend

Q:116=A

117. Who said 'I was married by a judge.
I should have asked for a jury'?

A: George Burns
B: George Bush
C: Basil Brush

Q:117=A

118. In which name should the
bride sign the register?

A: her new married name
B: her maiden name
C: a false name – just in case

Q:118=B

How did you score?
Check your scores below to find out...

Over 100

Congratulations! You've certainly done your homework (or you work for Confetti!). No one's catching you out on your wedding trivia. Whether it's obscure customs or handy quotations, you've got the information at your fingertips. We bet military manoeuvres aren't as well organized as your wedding!

Over 80

Not bad at all! There's very little about the wonderful world of weddings that you don't know. You're probably pretty much there with your big day but just need a few extra flourishes to give it that unique touch. Log on to www.confetti.co.uk for all those missing nuggets of information.